LUFTWAFFE AT WAR

Fighters Over Russia

P9-EKJ-233

By 1943 enemy action had rendered use of the Ju 87 very dangerous. *Luftwaffe* command therefore decided to use FW 190 fighter-bombers instead, and during autumn 1943 many Stuka-*Gruppen* were redesignated *Schlachtgruppen* under the command of a *Schlachtgeschwader*. Most of II/SG 2's aircraft, such as that pictured here, were FW 190F-3/R3s, which had been developed from a variant called an A-5/U17.

LUFTWAFFE AT WAR

Fighters Over Russia

Manfred Griehl

Greenhill Books
LONDON

Stackpole Books
PENNSYLVANIA

Greenhill Books

Fighters over Russia first published 1997
by Greenhill Books, Lionel Leventhal Limited,
Park House, 1 Russell Gardens,
London NW11 9NN
and
Stackpole Books, 5067 Ritter Road, Mechanicsburg,
PA 17055, USA

© Lionel Leventhal Limited, 1997
The moral right of the author has been asserted.

All rights reserved. No part of this publication may
be reproduced, stored in a retrieval system or trans-
mitted in any form or by any means, electronic,
mechanical or otherwise without first seeking the
written permission of the publisher.

British Library Cataloguing in Publication Data

Griehl, Manfred
Fighters over Russia. – (Luftwaffe at War; v. 1)
1. Germany. Luftwaffe – History – 20th century
2. World War, 1939–1945 – Aerial operations, German
I. Title
940.5'44'943
ISBN 1-85367-270-X

Library of Congress Cataloging-in-Publication Data

Griehl, Manfred
Fighters over Russia/Manfred Griehl.
72p. 26cm. – (Luftwaffe at war; v. 1)
ISBN 1-85367-270-X
1. Airplanes, Military – Germany – History.
2. Germany. Luftwaffe. 3. World War, 1939–1945 –
Campaigns – Eastern Front. 4. World War, 1939–1945
– Aerial operations, German. I. Title. II. Series.
UG1245.G4G753 1997   96-39872
940.54'4943 – DC21   CIP

Designed by DAG Publications Ltd.
Designed by David Gibbons.
Layout by Anthony A. Evans.
Edited by Ian Heath.
Printed and bound in Singapore.

The photographs in this book were taken under
wartime conditions. Some are not of the highest
quality, and are included because of their
extreme rarity.

FIGHTERS OVER RUSSIA

At the commencement of the Russian campaign, 22 June 1941, three well equipped *Luftflotten* (Air Fleets), numbers 1, 2 and 4, were ranged between the Baltic Sea in the north and Rumania in the south, boasting an impressive total of some 2770 aircraft; front-line combat aircraft strength, however, was a good deal less. *Luftflotte* 1 was commanded by an experienced officer, *Generaloberst* Alfred Keller. He was responsible for all operations of I *Fliegerkorps* (Air Corps), which was subordinated under the command of *Luftflotte* 1. Most of the Bf 109E day fighter units belonging to this formation — comprising I to III *Gruppen* of JG 54 and II *Gruppe* of JG 53 (JG standing for *Jagdgeschwader*, or Fighter Wing) — were based in East Prussia, having been allocated to support Army Group North, operating on the northern flank. The major responsibility of the fighters belonging to *Luftflotte* 1 was the protection of their own offensive Ju 88 bombers, which were used to carry out raids over the Baltic coast, Lithuania, Latvia and Estonia. *Luftflotte* 1's second *Fliegerkorps* was General Wolfram von Richthofen's VIII *Fliegerkorps*, stationed on assorted Polish airfields and equipped with Bf 109Fs. These belonged to parts of JG 27, 52 and 53. In addition there were the *Zerstörers* (destroyers) of *Zerstörergeschwader* (Destroyer Wing) ZG 26. *Luftflotte* 1's most important target was the region round Leningrad, one of the principal cities of the USSR.

Luftflotte 2, commanded by *Generalfeldmarschall* Albert Kesselring, was transferred to the Eastern Front to reinforce the capability of the other *Luftflotten*. Formerly most of its units had operated over Western Europe. In June 1941 it was proposed that *Luftflotte* 2 should operate between Minsk and Smolensk, being responsible for two different *Fliegerkorps*, numbers II and VII. *Luftflotte* 2 was well equipped, its formations possessing the best striking-power of any on the Eastern Front. Its fighter and destroyer units were JG 51 and I and IV/JG 53 (both equipped with Bf 109Fs), along with destroyers from the well-trained ZG 26.

Finally there was *Luftflotte* 4, commanded by *Generaloberst* Alexander Löhr, withdrawn from the Balkans and posted in Rumania and the southern part of occupied Poland. This *Luftflotte* was responsible for V and VI *Fliegerkorps*, which were to cover the southern part of the USSR, especially on the front between the Pripet Marshes and Rumania. The famous JG 3 and III/JG 52 were concentrated there.

In addition fighters of JG 77 and a few *Zerstörer* belonging to *Luftflotte* 5, isolated in the far north of occupied Norway, had also been preparing for action over Russia.

The entire German fighter strength consisted of 830 single-engine and some 90 twin-engine (*eg* Bf 110) destroyer aircraft. Of the *Luftwaffe*'s grand total of 4300 available combat aircraft, 2770 were concentrated on the borders of the USSR at the end of May 1941. Of these not less than 1500 belonged to *Luftflotte* 2, while *Luftflotte* 4 had some 760; the units operated by *Luftflotten* 1 and 5 were considerably smaller. They constituted just part of the German forces assembled to launch a massive *Blitzkrieg* (lightning campaign) against European Russia, their task being to provide direct and effective ground support for the *Wehrmacht* divisions moving against Leningrad, Moscow, and the Black Sea coast. The *Luftwaffe* units were well-equipped, their officers and men had confidence in the superiority of their aircraft and equipment, and everyone was convinced that the USSR's unconditional surrender would take place well before the end of 1941.

Together with the *Kampfgeschwader* (Bomber Wings), most day fighter units participated in the initial onslaught of German air power against the USSR, using small SD 2 fragmentation bombs. In addition Bf 110 units were used to destroy Russian bases far behind the front line. In the first days of the campaign German air-strikes achieved great success. Having completed the first phase of the operation, the single-engine fighters switched to close protection of the twin-engine bomber forces, mainly He 111s, operating over the central sector of the new Eastern Front. When *Luftwaffe* operations intensified over the northern sector, VII *Fliegerkorps* was subordinated to *Luftflotte* 1 in order to strengthen the close-support capability required for Ju 87 Stuka-equipped units. During the rapid advance towards Leningrad, the day fighters continued to protect the slower bomber forces on their way East, until Leningrad itself came under direct attack by the aircraft of *Luftflotte* 1.

During August 1941, motorised forces of the *Wehrmacht* made their way through the western Ukraine, with air support provided by *Luftflotte* 4. In consequence of the close protection provided by the fighters, *Luftwaffe* bombing operations against Kiev, and on harbours and shipping in the Black Sea, were everywhere successful, Ju 87 dive-bombers targeted against the latter having been escorted by modern Bf 109F-2 fighters belonging to JG 52. The Red Army's withdrawal in September 1941 persuaded the German High Command that the most critical phase of its lightning campaign was over. After Leningrad was placed under siege, it seemed all that remained to be done was to launch a final offensive against the Soviet capital, Moscow.

The *Luftwaffe* therefore adjusted its dispositions in the central sector. Since some 50% of all *Luftwaffe* forces on the Eastern Front were concentrated under *Luftflotte* 2, it was decided to redeploy VII *Fliegerkorps* back from *Luftflotte* 1, enabling most of the long-range He 111 bombers and the greater part of 400 single-engine Bf 109E and F fighters and heavy Bf 110 destroyer aircraft to be assigned ready for further offensive action.

The attack on Moscow opened on 1 October 1941 and within the first few days made considerable progress thanks to the combined air support provided by bombers, ground attack aircraft and even fighters. With the onset of winter, worsening weather conditions not only limited the number of air support missions that could be mounted, but reduced movement on the ground even more dramatically. Despite these disadvantages, however, German ground forces succeeded in pressing eastward as far as Kalinin and Vjasma before further bad weather, deep mud, and strengthening Russian opposition brought the *Wehrmacht*'s advance to a halt. By December 1941 the general conditions had deteriorated yet further, accompanied by a severe drop in temperature. Several fighters and bombers were damaged landing on the frozen runways of forward airfields, their undercarriages and tail-wheels breaking away; others suffered engine failure in action. The DB 601 engines of Bf 109E and F fighters suffered particularly badly, and could not be changed due to the poor maintenance facilities available on forward airstrips, situated close behind the front line.

Unfortunately for the *Luftwaffe*, well-equipped Russian fighter forces had been concentrated against them, backed up by Moscow's strong anti-aircraft defences. While German air support withered under the adverse weather conditions which lasted till the end of 1941, the Red Air Force was able to counter German attacks with numerous day fighter sorties, the *Luftwaffe* only being able to mount adequate air support over a few isolated parts of the Moscow front. While air superiority passed to the Russians, German ground forces were neutralised by a combination of freezing conditions and Red Army onslaughts. The attack on Moscow failed.

In the southern sector the lack of air support, with most fighter units being below strength, meant that the Germans were forced to pull back beyond their original positions. Russian fighter strength, by contrast, increased from 285 on 1 October to 674 on 5 December 1941.

During the ensuing winter campaign (1941–2) the number of understrength units in the central sector — mainly those with Bf 109F aircraft — increased, these belonging to JG 27, 51, 53 and 54. Of some 1700 aircraft, 1100 had been destroyed within just six months. Not expecting the *Blitzkrieg* to fail, *Luftwaffe* fighter forces on the Eastern Front were ill-prepared to face the severity of the Russian winter, lacking adequate accommodation, suitable clothing for the maintenance personnel, and the equipment necessary for overhauling their aircraft engines. The Red Air Force, meanwhile, was able to continue its own offensive actions against the small *Jagdgeschwader* airfields. Serviceability of German aircraft fell as low as 30–40%. In addition replacement Bf 109F-2 and F-4 aircraft did not become available in sufficient numbers in consequence of the demands for reinforcements made by fighter units based in Western Europe and the Mediterranean theatre, to compensate for the withdrawal of *Luftflotte* 2 and II *Fliegerkorps* for service in Russia.

The Russian winter offensive of 1941–2 began to threaten important centres behind the lines. As they pushed on towards Kharkov, Kursk and Smolensk, only limited *Luftwaffe* forces had been available to defend a few key positions. Unless air superiority was recovered by its own fighter forces, further withdrawals on the ground were inevitable. As many fighters as possible were therefore assigned to the protection of close-support forces, mainly Ju 87 dive-bombers, which continued low-level attacks on Soviet tanks and against positions on and behind the central sector.

Despite the severe weather conditions, German fighter units managed to improve their airfields in the middle and southern parts of Russia so as to be ready to resume offensive operations as soon as winter ended. However, in consequence of the ensuing thaw, which began in April 1942, most of these bases were rendered unusable on account of their muddy airstrips.

In order to get oil from the Caucasus, the main thrust of the new German offensive was planned to take place against the southern part of the front line, in the hope that the Russian war machine would be simultaneously cut off from its main source of oil. After the Crimea had been completely occupied, except for the city of Sebastopol, German forces moved into the southern part of the Caucasus, *Luftflotte* 4 and IV *Fliegerkorps* attempting to protect German positions against Russian attacks that were mounted during March 1942. Till June 1942 VIII *Fliegerkorps* was also engaged in the critical southern part of the front, while IV *Fliegerkorps* moved to positions near the Black Sea coast. Simultaneously with renewed attacks on Sebastopol, a Russian offensive directed against Kharkov resulted in more German forces being transferred to the battle front. In addition the *Luftwaffe* succeeded in getting more than 2700 aircraft into operation again, of which 1500 were deployed in South Russia under the command of *Luftflotte* 4. During this period only 600 combat aircraft, together with minimal fighter forces, operated in the central sector, while even fewer were placed in the north, on the Leningrad front, in northern Norway, and in Finland.

In July 1942 the *Wehrmacht* began a new offensive in southern Russia, against a Red Army defence whose air support — fighters, close-support aircraft, light and medium bombers — had been increased during the preceding few months. Despite a strong resistance and counter-attacks by the Red Army, the *Wehrmacht* reached the Volga at Stalingrad (Volgograd), one of the principal industrial centres of southern Russia. However, even after the arrival of German reinforcements, Stalingrad did not fall. On the other side of the front line more and more Russian divisions were concentrating behind the southern sector, and in October 1942 a counter-offensive began.

In the Middle Don region German air power was weak, only some 75 aircraft being available to cover a 500 km front. The advance of strong Red Army forces from the Don towards the south-west was so successful that the Germans were forced to retreat. Many forward airfields were overrun or abandoned, so that no close-support or single-seat fighter units were available. This gave Russia complete air superiority over a wide swathe of the battlefield including the ruins of Stalingrad, where the German 6th Army was encircled. During the first phase of the Russian operation only some 375 single-engine fighters were available to support German forces, especially for the protection of close ground-support attacks by Stukas and Heinkel bombers. The withdrawal of German forces soon became imperative. The distance between the front line and the besieged 'Stalingrad Army' steadily increased. In the end, despite massive efforts to keep the besieged city supplied using Ju 52 transport aircraft, the surrounded German forces were forced to surrender, the situation not having been helped by Hitler refusing his commander permission to retreat from the city.

Following the defeat of the 6th Army, a significant proportion of the *Luftwaffe*'s forces in Russia, in particular most of its newest fighters, was transferred to Libya and Tunisia, and activities in the Caucasus steadily decreased. Germany never again achieved air superiority on the Eastern Front. By February 1943 only 30% of all available day fighter forces were deployed in Russia, while 70% operated from bases round the Mediterranean or were involved in providing air cover over Western Europe. After the end of February 1943 more and more fighter aircraft, up to some 35% of the total available, were used for the defence of occupied Europe and in particular of the Reich itself.

After the defeat at Stalingrad and the withdrawal from the Caucasus, German forces had to retreat from other positions in the East. Russian divisions advanced to Voronezh on 16 February, and then Kharkov passed back into Russian hands. Because of the overwhelming strength of the enemy's forces *Luftflotte* 4 was unable to provide the necessary fighter support. Against all the odds, however, Kharkov was recaptured on 15 March during a German counter-offensive; but there was no chance of holding on to large parts of the Donets basin, even though more German ground forces had been concentrated there. In April 1943 a renewed German offensive was launched from the bridgehead of the Taman and Kuban peninsulas, aimed once more at the Caucasus region. On 17 April 1943 heavy attacks by more than 550 German aircraft were carried out, but the enemy proved strong enough to defend his positions and to halt the German offensive in its tracks. The German operation was aborted for want of supplies and manpower.

From the beginning of May 1943 preparations for a huge offensive against Kursk involved the transfer of VII *Fliegerkorps* to the Kharkov and Belgorod region. Also in May a new *Luftflotte* (number 6) was established in the central sector of the Russian Front, to cover the area between Smolensk and Orel along with the northern flank of the Kursk salient. By this time the *Luftwaffe* had stockpiled more than 2500 aircraft ready for the coming operation. Considering the heavy losses that had been suffered within the last six months, this was a remarkable recovery. Together with Ju 88 and He 111 bombers, ground-attack units called *Schlachtgruppen* (Battle Groups), newly equipped with FW 190 aircraft, were to take part. The fighter units were ordered to protect their offensive missions and to fly low-level attacks against Russian positions. In June 1943 the *Luftwaffe* opened the operation with 3000 sorties in the first day, but within eight days this figure had dropped to 1000, due to losses suffered at the hands of Russian fighters. Nor did the *Wehrmacht*'s achievements coincide with the High Command's plans, its attacks being contained by the great number of Russian entrenchments and fortifications which were encountered. By 5 August 1943, following a Russian counter-attack launched from the north on 15 July, the Kursk offensive had failed. Despite every serviceable German aircraft having been pressed into action, in the face of Russian air superiority there were simply not enough fighters available to interdict both the close-support and fighter operations of the enemy's forces. Therefore, without sufficient air cover, and having achieved only minor successes on the ground, the German divisions had begun to withdraw by the end of July 1943. On 4 August Russian troops liberated both Orel and Belgorod.

From this time on there was a radical change in the military situation. After the Orel salient was taken, the Red Army prepared to open its next offensive.

Following the failure of Germany's last major attack on the Eastern Front, between August and

December 1943 the Russians moved forward on the Dnieper. With the loss of Kharkov went its well-equipped airfields. From 27 August, Soviet ground forces had begun to overrun the whole area between Stalino (Donetsk) and Taganrog. German resistance received only minimal protection from its fighter units, the *Luftwaffe* units responsible for the central sector being still very weak, with only about 480 aircraft available to cover some 500 km of front line. This enabled the Russians to advance rapidly. Bryansk and Smolensk fell to the advancing Red Army by 25 September. In October they succeeded in obtaining bridgeheads on the west bank of the Dnieper River. At the end of October *Luftwaffe* attempts to destroy enemy forces concentrated at Krivoy Rog succeeded in halting the Russian advance only briefly. The progressive weakening of German ground and *Luftwaffe* forces alike resulted in a lack of significant counter-attacks in the Kiev region and the Pripet Marshes. On 6 November 1943 Russian forces broke through the German front line and reached Kiev. Then a rapid advance towards the city of Zhitomir was followed by desperate German counter-attacks. Some 75% of all German air power on the Eastern Front was employed, and minor tactical successes were achieved by concentrating on the vulnerable Russian spearheads. In addition the Crimea now came under threat from Russian forces, and the Red Air Force tried to interrupt coastal shipping lanes between the Crimea and Rumania, where only a few understrength fighter units were available to protect German vessels.

Due to an increasing need for more and more fighters in the West — to strengthen the *Reichsverteidigung* (protection of Germany) against Allied bombers — only a limited to poor supply of replacement fighters was made available to *Jagdgeschwader* stationed on the Eastern Front. Soviet fighter forces, however, equipped with American lend-lease material and the increasing output of their own production lines, were able to make good their losses within a very short time, though the training of new fighter pilots and commanding officers was more time-consuming. There was only one minor improvement to the German's own operational capabilities, with the arrival of the up-to-date FW 190A piston-engine fighter. This became available in only small numbers, however, most FW 190s being needed over Western Europe. The declining numbers of serviceable German fighter aircraft continued to keep them at a disadvantage.

By means of a huge outflanking movement, by March 1944 the Russian armies had started threatening the Rumanian oilfields essential to the German war machine. Therefore *Luftwaffe* bomber formations were concentrated at Vierine, and a few fighter units were withdrawn from the Balkans. Because there were two *Fliegerkorps* (I and VIII) in the Ukraine these too were ordered to support German ground forces in Rumania, as effectively as they could with the limited number of serviceable aircraft at their disposal.

The Soviet advance resulted in Germany's fighters losing many more of their airfields, not to mention a lot of experienced fighter pilots, and, not surprisingly, an even larger number of inexperienced ones. In May 1944 a reorganisation of the *Luftwaffe*'s forces in the East was necessitated by the enormity of its recent losses. Only some 700 to 750 front-line aircraft — 40% of all German aircraft in the Eastern theatre — had survived the Russian advance, these being concentrated in Poland and Bessarabia, while the air forces of Germany's allies, Rumania and Hungary, lacked the strength to provide any significant support. On 26 June 1944 most of the FW 190s available belonged to JG 54, while JG 51 and 52 were still equipped with Bf 109G aircraft, as were elements of JG 53 and JG 77, operating from Rumania.

It was not long before Soviet ground forces surged across occupied Poland to reach the borders of East Prussia, and overwhelmed Germany's Rumanian and Hungarian allies. Budapest had been outflanked early in December 1944, when divisions of the Red Army appeared before Warsaw's suburbs. By this time the number of German fighters available had dwindled to not more than 350 single-engine aircraft, operated by three *Luftflotten* (numbers 1, 4 and 6), of which *Luftflotte* 6 possessed nearly 200. There were also some 100 twin-engine destroyers and heavy destroyers, together with a few night fighters belonging to *Luftflotte* 6. Altogether not more than about 450 German fighter aircraft remained in the East by 1 January 1945, just one-sixth of the *Luftwaffe*'s operational Eastern Front strength as it had stood in June 1941. After this, final collapse and surrender became inevitable despite gallant stands in the last weeks of the war.

Above: A Bf 109 E 'White 11' of II/JG 54, handed over to a training unit after the first Bf 109F fighters had arrived in the Russian theatre. Because the ground at forward airfields was a different colour, the aircraft's earlier camouflage has been painted over with a darker mottled pattern to give it a better chance of surviving low level attacks by Red Army aircraft.

Below: This Bf 109F-4 fighter operated over the northern sector of the *Ostfront*, and in 1941 belonged to 7 *Staffel* of JG 54 'Grünherz'. During the attack on Russia JG 54 was subordinated under the command of I *Fliegerkorps* (*Luftflotte* 1) and was based at Kowno, Dünaburg and Ostrov. In August 1941 a significant part was redeployed in the Leningrad (St Petersburg) region.

The Romanian air force was equipped with fifty Bf 109Es, about twelve Bf 109Gs and several IAR 80 and PZL fighters. Of these more than 60% were lost in action over Russia and Romania. Altogether the *Corpul Aerian* (Romanian air command) comprised *Flotila* 2 Vanataori, in which there were eight fighter units, each of ten or twelve aircraft. Three of these units (*Esc.* 56 to 58) were equipped with Bf 109E fighters such as that shown here.

Two technicians of I/JG 52 working on the piston engine of one of the unit's Bf 109s. Regular maintenance was vital, so that as many aircraft as possible could be kept serviceable to counter the steady growth of Russian airpower.

Photographed in the winter of 1941/2, this 'White 2', a Bf 109F-2 of III/JG 53 'Pikas', is standing in the partial shelter of a bay of snow. Snow led to many Bf 109s — E, F and G models — being damaged in taking off and landing, increasing the *Luftwaffe*'s difficulties in finding sufficient aircraft to replace losses sustained in action.

At Kharkov-Roganj a day fighter of 1 *Staffel* of JG 52 awaits further action. This Bf 109G-6 'White 10' (s/n 19881) was flown by *Leutnant* Willmann in summer 1943. There was little chance of escape if Soviet low level attacks took place when the *Gruppe's* aircraft were caught isolated in the open like this.

Pilots sit in the cockpits of their FW 190s belonging to I/JG 54, ready to take off. Many of the Focke-Wulf fighters transferred to I *Gruppe* got a rather dark camouflage, and the yellow background to their fuselage *Balkenkreuz* insignia is characteristic of the Russian theatre.

Oberleutnant Gerhard Barkhorn — initially commanding officer of 4 *Staffel* II/JG 52, and subsequently of II *Gruppe* itself — and *Leutnant* Plücher, photographed on the airfield at Kharkov-Roganj. Barkhorn was awarded the Knight's Cross on 23 August 1942, plus Oak Leaves on 12 January 1943 and Swords on 2 March 1944.

Above: FW 190As of I/JG 54 flying over the Vyazma–Orel region on the lookout for interesting targets. In 1943 parts of this *Geschwader* were engaged in protecting the northern sector of occupied Russia against Soviet air raids. Early in 1943 the conversion of the unit to FW 190s took place at Heiligenbeil in East Prussia. It subsequently saw service in several parts of the Eastern Front.

Below: This Bf 109G-1 'White 10' of I/JG 52 is undergoing maintenance by its ground-crew on an airfield at Gostagayewskaya, north-east of Anapa in the southern part of *Heeresgruppe Süd* (Army Group South).

Above: III *Gruppe* of *Jagdgeschwader* 52 (III/JG 52) was commanded by *Major* Albert Blumensaat. His unit operated all
over the southern sector of the Eastern Front. The *Gruppe*
was initially equipped with Bf 109E single-seat fighter aircraft, with two MG FF 20 mm cannon in its wings.

Below: Only a short time after transfer to III/JG 52, this Bf
109E equipped with a 300-litre drop tank awaits new camouflage and markings before serving with a front line unit. The
KD+EJ constitutes the so-called *Stammkennzeichen* (or
Funkrufkennzeichen), the code letters of the aircraft applied
by the manufacturer.

Above: The pilot of PG+BO, a Bf 109E, lost his orientation and was forced to carry out a belly-landing near the former Polish frontier when flying with 7 *Staffel* (Squadron) of JG 54, which was engaged in action over the northern sector of the Eastern Front. During the first day of the 1941 German offensive the single-seat fighters were involved in low level attacks on Soviet air bases.

Below: In the opening days of the offensive the *Luftwaffe* made many successful attacks, damaging large numbers of Russian aircraft by means of fragmentation bombs. Thousands of more or less wrecked aircraft were captured as the *Wehrmacht* advanced towards Moscow. These U-P training aircraft were photographed towards the northern end of the theatre of operations.

Above: Many Polikarpov I-153 aircraft, improved variants of the slower I-15 and I-152 fighters, were found abandoned on the Soviet airfields hit by the *Luftwaffe* in June 1941. Only a small number remained fit for further service. Note bomb racks beneath the wings.

Right: The aircraft of *Oberstleutnant* Werner Mölders, who was awarded the Oak Leaves on 21 September 1940 for his forty victories and was commanding officer of JG 51. It is a fast Bf 109F fighter, which entered operational service in 1941. By October 1940 Mölders had already claimed five more air victories, and he was to bring his score up to 115 over Russia.

Above: A *Luftflotte* 2 Bf 109E, 'Black 8' of I/JG 52. This aircraft, operated by 2 *Staffel*, was lost due to pilot error when landing after having escorted Stukas attacking targets near the city of Kiev early in August 1941.

Left: This Bf 109F-2, 'Black 2', has seen many missions, and shows a faded camouflage scheme. 'Black 2' belonged to I/JG 52, which had received many early Bf 109F-1 fighters after handing over its Bf 109Es to other units, including training units based in the Reich.

Above: During the opening stages of the invasion of Russia several Bf 109Es were lost due to enemy action. Additional losses resulted from technical problems or pilot error behind enemy lines. Aircraft which crashed on their own side of the front line were retrieved by specially-equipped recovery units.

Below: These Bf 109F-2s belonged to 6 *Staffel* of II/JG 54. The latter had formerly been part of I/JG 138, which was later redesignated I/JG 76 before becoming II/JG 54. Most of 6 *Staffel*'s aircraft were very intensively camouflaged. Some pilots of II/JG 54 were engaged in successful low-level bombing raids, carrying an SC 250 bomb beneath the fuselage of each of their Bf 109F-2s and F-4s.

Above: In 1941, the *Kommodore* of JG 52, *Major* Hans Trübenbach, flew one of the new Bf 109F-4s (s/n 7090), which was manufactured by Wiener-Neustädter Flugzeugwerke (WNF) near Vienna in June 1941. Trübenbach's aircraft was photographed on October 1941 at Tiraspol. On the left side of it fuselage the triangle specifying 87 octane fuel for the aircraft's DB 603 E engine can be clearly seen.

Below: This is the aircraft of the commanding officer of II/JG 54, Dietrich Hrabak, who had scored some twenty-four of his eventual 125 victories by July 1941. The white parts of the *Balkenkreuz* have been daubed with dark green paint to improve its camouflage. Note the wing-root matting to protect the metal surface; this was discarded prior to take-off.

Right: Bf 109 variants differed mainly in their Daimler-Benz engines. Both the Bf 109F-1 and F-2 were equipped with a DB 601 N, while the F-4 had a more powerful piston engine, the DB 601 E. All of these engines required considerable attention to remain in operational condition. The photograph shows trained mechanics of JG 52 together with one of the so-called *Technischer Aussendienst* of Daimler-Benz, who provided a technical field service to maintain the fighter's engines.

Below: A maintenance service team of I/JG 52 rearming the cowling guns of a Bf 109F-4. Armament consisted of one 20 mm cannon and two MG 17s installed above the DB 601 piston engine. Only a few Bf 109Fs received MG 131 guns, which replaced the MG 17. A very rare variant, called the F-6, was armed with two additional MG FF fixed in both wings. Note the armoured plate to the rear of the pilot's canopy.

Top left: 'Black 13' was operated by *Hauptmann* Erich Woitke, who flew an F-2 before the first F-4 became available. Woitke became commanding officer of I/JG 52. *Hauptmann* Johannes Steinhoff took over command on 1 March 1942.

Bottom left: During the initial phase of the Russian campaign the Germans overran numerous Red Army airfields, where many aircraft had been abandoned intact due to lack of fuel or poor airfield conditions. This UT-I-16, a highly manoeuvrable two-seat trainer, was later used by the *Luftwaffe* for its own training purposes.

Above: The suddenness of Germany's offensive was responsible for heavy losses of Soviet aircraft on the ground. Despite the fact that many seem to have suffered minimal damage, no attempt was made to find further operational use for the greater number of the aircraft that were captured.

Below: This Russian SB-2 M100 medium bomber was found on a small Red Air Force base near Pleskau in summer 1941. A limited number of these aircraft were taken over by the *Luftwaffe* for target-towing and liaison duties over Europe. Others were employed in pilot training.

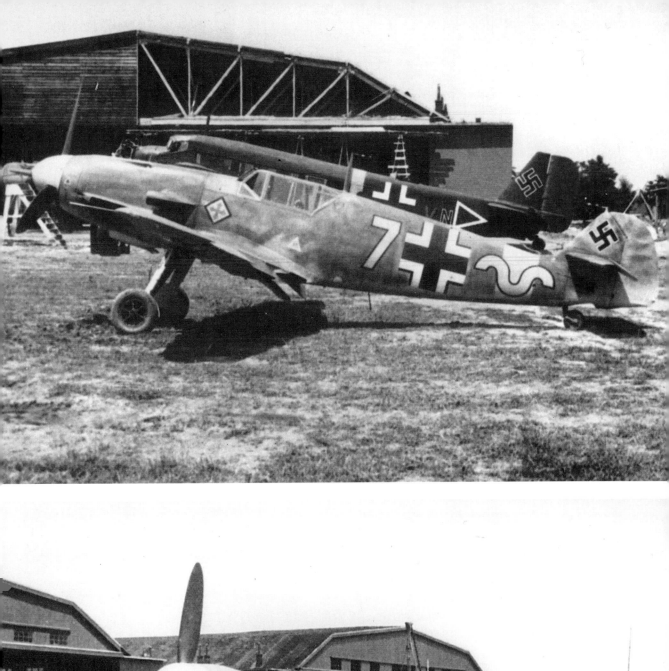

Opposite page: This 'White 7', a Bf 109F-4, belonged to III/JG 52 and saw action over the northern sector of the Eastern Front. It was manufactured by WNF and is fitted with an early version of an air intake on the left side of its DB 601 piston engine. The Ju 52 standing behind it in the first picture shows a large black/white triangle on the rear of its fuselage.

Above: After a final all-out offensive against Moscow had failed in the face of fierce Russian resistance, the *Luftwaffe* had to endure its first Russian winter. Several units were withdrawn from their forward airfields, back to bases captured from the enemy. This Bf 109F of JG 54 found shelter in one of the large hangars found still standing at Krasnogvardeyskoye.

Above: A lot of manpower was required to clear the runways and taxiways after heavy falls of snow had paralysed *Luftwaffe* activity on most of its forward air strips during the hard winter of 1941–2. The lack of warm clothes for its mechanics, and of 'warm-up' systems for the aircraft, severely affected aircraft maintenance. Consequently serviceability fell as low as 30% in most units.

Below: Although many *Luftwaffe* fighter units had been withdrawn to rear positions, a few *Staffeln*, such as those of I/JG 54, continued in action over the Eastern Front, especially during the Russian winter offensive which threatened German positions in the central sector. Well-equipped enemy forces succeeded in taking Rostov and subsequently threatened Kharkov.

Above: There were several experiments aimed at improving fighter performance on the Eastern Front. This Bf 109F-2 (s/n 8195, VD+AJ) belonged to a batch of 172 early F-series aircraft which were produced at Erla near Leipzig. One of these was tested with ski landing-gear called *Schneekufen* (snow skids). In January 1941 the first trials with a modified Bf 109E had ended with it crashing after some eighty successful flights.

Below: This FW 190A-2 (RI+KW) was similarly tested with ski landing-gear in Norway early in 1941. However, the reduced performance resulting from air resistance caused by the skis prevented their introduction on single-seat fighters and heavy destroyers. Consequently only Ju 52 transports were fitted with ski landing-gear.

Top left: Many fighter units based behind the Eastern Front operated their own *Jabo* (*Jagdbomber*, or fighter-bomber) units. One of these belonged to II/JG 54, which was mainly engaged in offensive action and close-support missions to relieve the pressure on German ground forces. Bf 109E-4/B aircraft with both MG FF removed from the wings were fitted with two or four SC 50 bombs, as here.

Bottom left: II *Schlachtgruppe* of *Lehrgeschwader* (Training Wing) 2 was partly equipped with BF 109E-7/B fighter-bombers, which were engaged in ground support operations using ETC 500 bombs fixed beneath the main fuselage. This aircraft is awaiting further action with one SC 250 bomb in place. Note the eyes and teeth chalked on the bomb.

Above: Their restricted performance meant that it was necessary to provide protection for the fighter-bombers in action. Preparing to take off as part of 3 *Staffel* of I/JG 51, this FW 190A-6 is heavily armed with four 20 mm weapons installed in the wings and two more fixed MG 131 guns above the radial engine. In addition to close protection missions, the Focke-Wulfs were used to intercept enemy intruders.

Below: The Ilyushin Il-2 Sturmovik was a heavily armed and well armoured Russian low level attack plane, which was used to support ground forces and to destroy German supply lines. This one was shot down near Pleskau by fighters belonging to JG 54.

Above: Only a few Il-2s were captured in flying condition. This Sturmovik in German markings was used to teach German pilots and anti-aircraft gunners the less armoured parts of the airframe. This is an early production model single-seater, and therefore lacks the rear-cockpit heavy machine-gun common to the later two-seat models.

Left: This Bf 109G was operated by Spanish volunteers who had formed two fighter *Staffeln* in 1941. The first was commanded by *Comandante* Angel Salas, the second by *Capitán* Noriega, who was killed in action on 1 July 1942. Afterwards *Comandante* Salas was ordered to take command. By November 1942 the unit had flown more than 400 fighter missions and achieved some thirteen confirmed victories. In addition 779 escort missions were carried out.

Right: The stiff canvas cover over the nose of this Bf 109G-2 of JG 52 was to protect its piston engine from dust and dirt. At various times during German counter-offensives, several missions were flown per day. The superhuman efforts of the technicians — who were nicknamed 'black men' on account of their black overalls — in keeping their charges airborne meant that they sometimes fell asleep in the strangest places.

Below: With the failure of the attack on Moscow, all available *Luftwaffe* aircraft were ordered to stop the subsequent Russian counter-offensive. However, only a limited number of bombers, such as this He 111 H-4 of II/KG 55, escorted by a few serviceable Bf 109 fighters, could get into action on account of the adverse weather conditions.

Left: Two specialists belonging to the ground crew of JG 54 prepare a Bf 104F-4 for action. The shell ammunition for the 20 mm gun consisted of two different types of grenade heads, purely explosive shells being combined with incendiary shells fitted with an additional explosive load. It was also possible to arm the MG 151/20 or MG FF with fragmentation or armour-piercing ammunition.

Above: This Bf 109F, 'Yellow 9', belonged to 9 *Staffel* of JG 54, and was flown over Russia in March 1942. On the side of the engine cowling can be seen the unit's devil's-head emblem.

Below: *Hauptmann* Günther Scholz inspecting his aircraft. In 1942 he was the commanding officer of III/JG 5, which was ordered to protect the northern sector of the Eastern Front. Later Scholz was promoted to *Oberstleutnant* and claimed some twenty victories in the air. Between February and May 1945 he became *Geschwaderkommodore* of JG 5 and simultaneously was appointed to be *Jagdfliegerführer* in Norway.

Left: This picture provides some idea of the poor conditions under which elements of III/JG 51 were forced to operate their Bf 109F-2s. After *Oberstleutnant* Werner Mölders was killed in an accident in 1942, this unit was named *Jagdgeschwader* Mölders. The unit was subordinated to *Luftwaffenkommando Ost* and operated largely from Dugino, near Reshew.

Right: The young *Oberleutnant* posing in front of his 'Black 1', a Bf 109F-4, was the commanding officer of 8 *Staffel* of JG 54. His aircraft belonged to a late production batch of F-4-fighters, recognisable by the larger air intake. In addition these aircraft were fitted with thick, bullet-proof glass in the front portion of the cockpit. The badge on the forward part of the cowling, representing a small bird, was that of 8 *Staffel*; the shield forward of the cockpit, with three aircraft over a cross, indicates III *Gruppe*; and the large green heart denotes JG 54.

Above: In summer 1942 these Bf 109F-4s were part of the *Geschwaderstab* (Staff Squadron) of JG 51, which was located on a seemingly endless meadow behind the northern part of the Eastern Front's central sector. The aircraft in the foreground was flown by the *Geschwader* Ia, the officer responsible for tactical operations. The one behind it belonged to the *Geschwader-Adjutant*.

Right: In the far north there were only small numbers of fighters belonging to JG 5, which, in addition to defending Finland and occupied Norway, were called on to protect the north-east sector of the Eastern Front. Because so few aircraft were available, and because the enemy's air superiority was so great, it was important that camouflage should be as effective as possible.

Above: The responsibility for painting new aircraft belonged to the each ground crew. These 'black men' are using a large stencil to spray the black-and-white *Balkenkreuz* over this aircraft's overall bright blue surface.

Left: The lack of a hangar or large shed left these mechanics having to perform the maintenance on a DB 601 N engine out in a snowy field. Because no winter uniforms were available the men tried to protect themselves from the bitter cold with scarves and woollen wrappers. In addition many ground crews wore two sets of underwear beneath their working suits.

Above: Regardless of bad weather and freezing temperatures, the robust Ju 52 transport aircraft maintained contact with positions to the rear and flew in vitally needed spare parts and drums of aviation fuel to isolated forward airfields. This Ju 52 is having warm air pumped into its engines to keep them from freezing. Without such heaters even these reliable aircraft became unserviceable.

Below: Only with the help of easy-going Panje horses were JG 54's ground crews able to keep their aircraft refuelled during the Russian winter. These sleigh-horses were also used to transport ammunition, supplies and wood to *Luftwaffe* bases. The aircraft in the background, standing in front of a hangar taken over from the Red Army, is an FW 190A-4, operated by the *Gruppen-Adjutant* of I *Gruppe*.

Above: After 15 February 1942, I/JG 54 'Grünherz' was commanded by *Hauptmann* Hans Philipp, who had been awarded the Knight's Cross on 22 October 1940. He flew 500 missions, and shot down 206 aircraft, 178 of them on the Eastern Front. On 1 April 1943 he became *Kommodore* of JG 1, and was shot down near Nordhorn the same month after destroying a B-17 bomber.

Below: The 'White 20', a FW 190A-6, was flown by *Hauptmann* Wettstein, commanding officer of 5 *Staffel* II/JG 54, which was responsible for the protection of Ju 87 dive-bomber units such as that seen flying overhead. Though it managed to fly a large number of such missions, the *Luftwaffe* on the Eastern Front was too weak for them to be effective, most of the new aircraft manufactured being needed for the defence of the Reich.

Top right: In 1943 three *Staffeln* of III/JG 54 operated over the middle sector of the Eastern Front under the command of *Luftflotte* 4. On such muddy, unsurfaced airfields as that depicted here, broken landing-gear became commonplace. Numerous Bf 109s, but fewer FW 190s, suffered damage during take-off or landing.

Bottom right: Taken early in 1943, this photograph depicts a FW 190A-4, 'White 11' of I/JG 51, operating from a dirty, partly flooded airfield somewhere in Russia. Pilots had to handle their fighter aircraft with extreme care when manoeuvring across such airfields, since there was already enough for ground crews to cope with after every mission without having to worry about damaged undercarriages.

Above: During the winter of 1943 more and more FW 190 fighters were transferred to the Eastern Front to strengthen the *Luftwaffe*'s capabilities. On the enemy's side, increasing numbers of high-performance fighter aircraft became operational, enabling the Red Army to provide considerable protection for its offensive missions against the weakened *Luftwaffe*. Possibly this FW 190A-4 of I/JG 54 belonged to 3 *Staffel*, which suffered many losses early in 1943.

Below: The fighters of JG 51, 52 and 54 were ordered to protect bombers such as this He 111H-6, of *Luftflotte* 4, which was part of a unit operating over the southern part of the Russian Front in 1943. Owing to the seriousness of the situation on the ground, many Heinkel bombers were actually used for supply missions instead of offensive bombing raids.

Above: Although Ju 88A-4 bombers had a better performance record than the He 111H-6, the latter aircraft were only used in small numbers. Like the Heinkel bomber, the four-seat Junkers needed protection by well-trained fighter pilots. The Ju 88A-4 pictured belonged to KG 3, of which two *Gruppen* flew combat missions under the command of *Luftwaffenkommando* Don.

Right: *Kommodore* Werner Mölders in the cockpit of his Bf 109F. Notice the thick armoured glass of the windshield.

Top left: This Bf 109G-6 (VN+PR), together with another Messerschmitt, both equipped with one 300-litre drop tank, have interrupted their flight to Russia at Veszprem in Hungary. Both aircraft are still in a colour scheme sprayed by the manufacturing firm. Note the large *Balkenkreuze* situated on both the wings and the fuselage sides.

Bottom left: In summer 1943 a thirteenth *Staffel* had joined JG 51. The personnel were volunteers raised for Slovakian units, which had been allies of the *Wehrmacht* during the first years of the Russian campaign. The most successful Slovakian pilots were Sergeant-Major Jan Reznák (thirty-three victories), Staff Sergeant Izidor Kovarik (twenty-nine victories) and First Lieutenant Ján Gerthover (twenty-seven victories).

Above and below: These Yak 3 fighters were part of the Red Air Force's Normandie-Niemen Squadron, formed from French volunteers to support the Russians in their struggle against the *Luftwaffe*. The squadron was part of the 303 IAD during 1943–5. Some of the aircraft bore a cross of Lorraine on the tail fin. The ground crews were Russian.

Above: Major General A.A. Kuznetsov, the commanding officer of the Northern Fleet, before taking off. His aircraft, a Hawker Hurricane Mk IIB (s/n Z5252), saw action over Murmansk harbour in October 1941 after being handed over to the Red Army by 81 Squadron RAF. For his part in the defence of the northern approaches and harbours Kuznetsov had become a highly-decorated officer by 1945.

Left: Somewhere to the rear of the northern sector, a Bf 109F-2 of III/JG 54 stands ready for action in 1942. Because of heavy losses only a limited number of German fighters were available to defend their supply lines to the Baltic and eastern Poland. However, Soviet pilots failed to profit from their strength and did not press home their advantage.

Above: There was little free time for the 'black men' to relax. Even this ground-crew of I/JG 52, photographed behind the central sector in late summer 1943, seems to be involved in filling out a report, probably about the dire spare parts situation. Boxes and barrels substitute for furniture. Note the fire extinguisher, of a type used by all front-line units.

Below: A ground-crew of 1 *Staffel* of JG 52 try to overhaul a DB 601 E-1 piston engine removed from one of the unit's Bf 109F-4 fighters, supported on a crude stand. On the left side of the 990 kW engine the supercharger is easily recognisable. The gun integrated into the rear part of the engine had to be partly removed for maintenance work to be carried out.

Above: During the summer of 1942 II/JG 52 operated from bases in the southern sector. The spinner of this 'Yellow 6' (the number barely visible on the fuselage side), a Bf 109G-2 belonging to this *Gruppe*, has been removed during an inspection.

Below: In summer 1942 II/JG 51 was equipped with Bf 109F-2 and F-4 piston-engined fighters. To avoid being caught unprepared by Russian low-level attacks, many German units set up light anti-aircraft weapons or MG 34 machine-guns near accommodation areas.

Above: Several tents were needed to accommodate the technical ground-crew. Often there were too few, and no large ones in which difficult work could be done. Consequently there was often no chance for material testing, or for large-scale repairs to be carried out, because of a shortage of repair trucks and special equipment. Training and experience, however, enabled the mechanics to keep many of their aircraft serviceable.

Below: Only a few of the bases that had been formerly used by the Red Army were both well-equipped and captured relatively intact. The airfield of Pleskau, photographed here, was amongst those which had the machine-tools, the capacity, and the skilled personnel — belonging to one of the *Feldwerftkompanien* or *Feldwerftabteilung* — to carry out even complicated repair work within a short time.

Above: A view inside a large hangar on the Eastern Front. Only a few of these were available anywhere near the front line. Badly damaged aircraft were therefore scrapped and cannibalised for their spare parts, or were destroyed before units were forced to withdraw to rearward positions. The FW 190A in the foreground was flown by a *Major beim Stab* (Staff Major).

Below: Every *Luftwaffe* fighter unit was equipped with one or two small liaison aircraft to keep in touch with rear bases and to collect urgently-needed spare parts. In 1944 this Bf 108 belonged to JG 54, which was responsible for air defence over the northern sector. The Bf 108 was powered by an Argus As 10 C engine, rating 240 HP. It could carry three passengers plus the pilot.

Above: Coming under the command of *Luftflotte* 2, II/JG 52's *Staffeln* flew Bf 109Fs over the central sector of the Russian Front in late-1941. However, some units of JG 52 were subsequently re-equipped with FW 190 fighters, after which II *Gruppe* was transferred to southern Italy.

Below: On 13 August 1943 I/JG 27 was sent to Fels am Wagram to defend the south-east against bombers of the American 15th Air Force, which were threatening the Rumanian oil industry and the *Wehrmacht*'s supply lines. The aircraft shown belonged to the Bf 109G-6 series and was flown with one 300-litre drop tank fixed under the fuselage to extend its range.

Above: The Red Army succeeded in introducing more and more modern fighters thanks to the output of its large aircraft factories beyond the Ural mountains. This MiG-3 belonged to the Baltic Fleet and was captured with others by the *Wehrmacht* during a local offensive in 1942. A few were tested by the *Luftwaffe* at Rechlin, where aircraft evaluation was carried out.

Below left: This Bf 109G-3 was flown by III/JG 3 in 1943. The unit was under the command of VIII *Fliegerkorps*, being needed for the protection of occupied southern Russia and the Crimea. Due to its narrow landing-gear the Bf 109 suffered numerous losses during the Russian campaign, where rough landing strips often caused the undercarriage to break off, damaging both fuselage and wings in the process. Because of a lack of facilities to carry out extensive repair work such damaged aircraft frequently had to be blown up.

Right: *Unteroffizier* (NCO) Heinrich Blaut was the pilot of this Bf 109G-2 (s/n 14513) of JG 3 'Udet'. The colours of fighter aircraft were changed in April 1943 to improve camouflage. Blaut disappeared on 8 December 1942. Since his aircraft fell into Russian hands undamaged it seems likely that he landed on a Soviet airfield by mistake, or at least force landed undamaged.

Below: In July 1943, JG 52's 2 *Staffel* operated from a small airfield near Belgorod. Most of its aircraft belonged to the Bf 109G-6/R6 series and were equipped with two additional MG 151/20 guns below the wings. Besides being employed as heavily-armed fighters these Bf 109s were used for low level attacks against Soviet ground forces. Note that all the aircraft in the photograph carry drop tanks..

Above: Along with other aircraft of the unit, this Bf 109G-2, 'White 1' (*Oberleutnant* Hans Götz) of 7 *Staffel* III/JG 54, was photographed after landing in Finland on 6 June 1942. Based at the northern end of the Eastern theatre, 4 *Jagdbomber-Staffel* (Fighter-bomber Squadron) of JG 4 was engaged in low level raids under the command of *Luftflotte* 1. Götz achieved 82 victories during the war

Below: On 1 March 1943 several FW 190A-5s of II/JG 54 such as this, together with I/SG 3 and I/SG 5, formed the *Gefechtsverband* Kuhlmey, which operated from Immonola airfield in Finland under the command of *Luftflotte* 5 and was responsible for concentrated low level assaults against advancing Soviet armoured divisions. In September 1944 the unit was withdrawn after co-operation with Finland ended.

Above: Significant elements of I to III/JG 77 saw action over Rumania and Russia in 1944. *Fahnenjunker-Oberfeldwebel* Johann Pichler (right) belonged to III/JG 77, and became a prisoner of war on 30 August 1944. He was awarded the Knight's Cross on 7 September 1944, having shot down a total of seventy-five enemy aircraft, twenty-nine of them Russian.

Below: One of the major duties of *Jagdgeschwader* over the Eastern Front was the escort of Ju 87D and G dive-bombers. This Ju 87D-5 revving up on a snow-covered airfield is loaded with three bomb containers. Without adequate fighter protection, the slow Stukas often fell victim to LAAG and MiG fighters and suffered heavy losses.

Left: Maintenance of a DB 605 AM piston engine and cooling system, which has been removed from a Bf 109G-6 by means of a simple tripod-and-winch arrangement. This kind of engine enabled the fighter to fly at 544 km/h near to the ground, or at 623 km/h at an altitude of some 6500 m. The aircraft in the picture possibly belonged to JG 52.

Below: A tiny white '8' is barely visible in the angle of the double chevron painted on the fuselage of *Hauptmann* Walter Nowotny's FW 190A-6 (s/n 410004). Fighter ace Nowotny received the Diamonds to the Swords and Oak Leaves of his Knight's Cross on 19 October 1943. He was killed in action in 1944, flying a Me 262A-1a jet fighter.

Above: This Bf 109G was flown by *Hauptmann* Reinhard Seiler, the *Gruppenkommandeur* of III/JG 54, who was awarded the Knight's Cross on 20 December 1941 and the Oak Leaves on 2 March 1944. His unit was subsequently withdrawn from Russia to join the *Reichsluftverteidigung* (defence of the Reich). The two 'black men' are about to 'wind-up' the engine.

Below: This Bf 109F was operated from an airfield situated near Reshev, being involved in protecting German supply lines against massive Soviet strikes launched by the well-armoured Il-2 low-level attack aircraft. The ground-crew are waiting for the command to start up the DB 601 piston engine by means of a crank handle.

Above: A Bf 109G-6 of I/JG 3 'Udet' awaits its next mission on a waterlogged airfield. Despite the difficulties presented by mud, dirt and appalling weather conditions, every effort was made to keep sufficient aircraft serviceable for the *Luftwaffe* to keep fighting.

Below: The same conditions were to be found at every airfield of *Luftflotte* 4, all over southern Russia. This Ju 88A-4 combat aircraft, possibly belonging to I/KG 1, stands in a sea of mud early in 1943. Compared with the more robust He 111H-6, H-11 and H-20, only a few Ju 88 formations were posted to Russia in support of German units falling back to their own border.

Right: This FW 190 of I/JG 51 was lost in an landing accident. Being beyond repair, it would be stripped of all salvageable parts and abandoned, no explosives being available to destroy it. In this condition it eventually fell into Russian hands.

Below: Many Bf 109G-6s lost during the Russian campaign were recovered, like this one, by the Red Army, and saw limited service as training aircraft, or else underwent evaluation tests. A few of these piston-engine fighters were possibly handed over to the *Nationales Kommitee für ein Freies Deutschland* (the NKD), consisting of German prisoners who had opted to support the Soviet authorities. There were certainly reports by *Luftwaffe* pilots who believed they had seen German single-seat fighters with red stars painted on both wings and fuselage.

Right: A Bf 109G of 12 *Staffel* IV/JG 52, shown in Russian hands at
Chuyevo in July 1943. Possibly its Croatian pilot had surrendered to the
Red Army, handing his aircraft over to the 9th Guards IAP. This particular
aircraft was subsequently tested by the regimental commanding officer,
Major Lev L. Shestakov, who was killed in action on 13 March 1944.

Below: Despite Russian low level attacks and bombing raids, numerous
FW 190 fighters and fighter-bombers remained in flyable condition, ready
to go into action once bomb craters on the runways had been filled by
Luftwaffe ground-crews or Russian POWs. The aircraft shown belonged to
1 *Staffel* of SG 3, and was used during the Battle of Kursk.

Lower right: A pilot and members of his ground-crew look for the cause
of an engine failure. The aircraft belongs to JG 52, which was earned its
6000th victory by *Oberleutnant* Paul-Heinrich Dähne on 7 July 1943. He
had shot down ninety-nine (or possibly 100) enemy aircraft, and was
awarded the Knight's Cross on 6 April 1944 after destroying seventy-four
aircraft while serving with JG 52.

Above: This well-armoured FW 190G-2 belonging to an unknown unit could be fitted with three bombs or three bomb containers. Alteration of FW 190A-5/U8 to G-2 standards began early in January 1943 at one of the Focke-Wulf factories. The FW 190G-3, in production from July 1943, was the first entirely new G-series variant.

Below: The tents of an unknown 7 *Staffel* rest area (hiegeplatz) photographed in summer 1944. The tripod-mounted MG 15 in the foreground stood little chance of shooting down attacking aircraft. By 1944–5 it took at least a triple MG 151 to destroy Sturmoviks mounting low level raids.

Above: This 'White 2' belonged to II/JG 3 'Udet', equipped with Bf 109F-2s and F-4s before getting its first Bf 109G-1 fighters. By the end of the war the unit was flying Bf 109G-10s and was due to have received the more powerful K-4 variant by summer 1945, though by May only a handful had been delivered. It had even been planned to replace these with K-6 *Sturm* fighters as rapidly as possible.

Below: Early in 1945, JG 1 was equipped with both FW 190A-8s and A-9s and the Bf 109G-14/AS. In addition a limited number of Bf 109G-6s were used for training purposes. The aircraft shown being presented to a new pilot was produced by Wiener Neustädter. Because such novice pilots had only a small chance of surviving more than two or three missions, they were called *Dreitageflieger* (three-day flyers).

Top left: This Bf 109G-6 belonged to 9 *Staffel* of JG 1, commanded by *Oberst* Walter Oesau. He had previously been commanding officer of III/JG 51 and III/JG 3, both of which had operated over Russia. He shot down 125 aircraft in total, including eight over Spain and some forty-four over central Russia.

Bottom left: During their close co-operation with German day fighter units, Rumanian pilots were often engaged in air defence operations side-by-side with their allies. Most of the Rumanian units were equipped either with IAR 80 fighters or Bf 109G-4s. This photograph depicts one of several captured I-16s which, along with other Russian aircraft, had been taken over for use in training and air defence duties during 1942-3.

Top: On 8 February 1945 three *Gruppen* of JG 51 were equipped with Bf 109G-14 piston-engined fighters, only a few of them G-14/AS. The *Geschwader* was subordinated under the command of *Luftflotte* 6, and it was intended to change its equipment from G-14s to K-4s which, it was promised, would be available not later than June 1945. The aircraft in the photograph has a so-called Erla-Haube cockpit canopy, which gave the pilot improved visibility.

Above: A close-up view of the Erla-Haube cockpit canopy as fitted to many Bf 109G variants. Besides the Bf 109G-6, G-10 and G-14, all K-variants (K-1 to K-6) built before Germany's unconditional surrender were also fitted with this type of hood. A thick armour plate was installed behind the pilot's seat to provide protection against attacks from the rear.

Left: A few Bf 109G-6/U4s and some K-4/U4s were rebuilt to allow for the installation of two bulges, each housing a heavy MK 108 gun. The belt shown being held by a member of the ground-crew was used to pull the ammunition into its storage space within both wing sections. Note the massive grenade heads on each shell. The explosive power of just one or two of these shells was believed sufficient to destroy a heavy bomber.

Above: At first the monstrous Russian KV-2 tank was invulnerable to anything less than an 88 mm Flak gun, or a direct hit from an SD bomb. However, by the end of the war the *Luftwaffe* had introduced several rocket-assisted air-to-ground missiles which were capable of destroying a KV-2 or a Josef Stalin tank with a single direct hit. Consequently many FW 190s were rebuilt to carry eight to twelve or more such anti-tank rockets beneath the wings.

Top right: An FW 190F-8 of SG 2 is guided along a snow-covered runway at Sopoc. Under the fuselage is fixed a single wooden AB 500 bomb container. These were designed to house assorted combinations of explosives for use against concentrations of armoured vehicles, each AB 500 housing a load of small but formidable SD-1, SD-4 or SD-10 bomblets. During FW 190 operations against ground targets a few Bf 109G-10s, G-14s or K-4s were often detailed to provide protection against enemy fighters.

Bottom right: During winter 1944–5 this FW 190F-8 taxis to its take-off position with the help of its ground-crew, who are trying to control the aircraft's direction on the slippery surface. The fighter-bomber is loaded with one large SC 250 or SC 500 fragmentation bomb. It could also carry four SC 50s, SD 50s or SD 71s on the wings (note racks).

Top left: This FW 190F-8/R1 — abandoned by the *Luftwaffe* at Pardubice, east of Prague, through lack of either spare parts or fuel — was captured by Soviet forces at the end of April 1945. Scattered round it are a few SD 71 bombs and an empty AB 250 container.

Bottom left: At the end of 1944, III/JG 77 'Herz As' (Ace of Hearts) was equipped with Bf 109K-4 fighters. On 1 January 1945 this 'White 17', a K-4 (s/n 330230) of 9 *Staffel*, is being prepared for further action. Early in 1945 the *Geschwaderstab* and three *Gruppen* belonged to *Luftflotte* 6, and were stationed at Beneschau.

Above: Because of advances in Soviet fighter design it became necessary at the end of 1944 to introduce the 'long-nose' FW 190D-9, usable as both a day fighter and a fighter-bomber. The D-9 depicted belonged to 9 *Staffel* III/JG 54. Much of its camouflage cover has been removed so that the aircraft can be worked on in preparation for its next mission.

Below: At the end of the war much-depleted *Luftwaffe* units tried to stem the Soviet advance. Together with other *Jagdgeschwader*, II/JG 300 was engaged in protecting the thinly-defended Oder line, where understrength *Wehrmacht* ground forces, along with *Volkssturm* militia units, desperately tried to prevent Russian forces from entering central Germany and threatening the *Reichshauptstadt*.

Top left: This FW 190D-6/R5 could be fitted with four ETC 71 bombs, one ETC 502 and a so-called *Einheitsschloss*, on which all kind of bombs could be fitted. The aircraft belonged to JG 300, operating on the Eastern Front late in the war.

Bottom left: JG 6 was subordinated under the command of *Luftflotte* 6 and during February 1945 carried out sixty-seven missions with altogether 318 fighter aircraft. Of these 246 were FW 190 D-9 'Doras'. The aircraft shown is fitted with a 300-litre drop tank. Reports written at the time mention that Russian pilots often turned back if they encountered 'Doras'.

Above: This Bf 109G was captured by Czech insurgents near Prague-Kbely during the rising against the Germans at the beginning of May 1945. The aircraft had been isolated on the airfield and was abandoned when the Germans withdrew to Saaz and Pilzen. This aircraft was possibly taken over by the Allies.

Right: This Bf 109K-4 (s/n 334175) belonging to III/JG 51 has just taken off from Junkertroylhof, situated in the besieged East Prussia pocket, where thousands of refugees waited to be shipped to Schleswig-Holstein. A lack of fuel and spare parts rendered the defence of German positions in Kurland and East Prussia quite impossible as the advancing Russians progressively eliminated all resistance.

Above: Since the end of April 1945 many Bf 109K-4s belonging to surviving elements of JG 52 and JG 77 had been concentrated on airbases around Prague, where this destroyed aircraft was photographed. In addition Me 262A-1a jet fighters were ordered in to help defend the area, where a lot of German ground and *Luftwaffe* forces, together with *Armeegruppe* Schörner, were encircled by several Allied armies.

Below: These FW 190D-9s, photographed near Marienburg in East Prussia, have been taken over by the Soviet authorities. Possibly they represent the output of a local assembly line. The final fate of these fighters is still unknown.